THE POETRY OF COMPASSION

PROFESSOR PATRICK PIETRONI

FRESCO BOOKS

CONTENTS

COMPASSION AND THE OTHER

It is in the safety of
my own quiet corner
that I can acknowledge
my own shadow

Filled as it is with
all the blocks and hurdles
that limit my capacity
for compassion
to the other.
My shadow is my own other.

Know it
befriend it
you will find it
possible
to approach all the others
you will meet
on your own
journey
with compassion.

Patrick Pietroni

INTRODUCTION

The study of compassion has recently become a major academic discipline. There is an academic saying, "It is impossible to say everything that can be said about a topic". This is certainly true about compassion, but I have found that poetry manages to do a very good job and I trust that this little volume will provide a helpful companion to the many academic texts now also available.

In Charles Darwin's first book *The Expression of Emotion in Man and Animals*[1] he explored whether other animals demonstrated the same facial expression as we do — anger, surprise, sadness, fear, etc. Modern Darwinism is now equally studying whether other species exhibit compassionate behaviour as well. In his last book *The Decent of Man*,[2] Darwin wrote:

> *"Sympathy beyond the confines of man, that is, humanity to lower animals, seems to be one of the latest moral acquisitions... This virtue, one of the noblest with which man is endowed, seems to arise incidentally from our sympathies becoming more tender and more widely diffused until they extend to all sentient beings."*

Darwin's theory of evolution by natural selection is the cornerstone of our modern understanding of both human and non-human origins and development. In his three major works: *On the Origin of Species*[3], *The Expression of the Emotions in Man and Animals*, and *The Descent of Man*, it is possible to trace his understanding of the evolutionary nature of compassion and empathy, although he refers to these qualities in terms of "sympathy", "moral actions" and "social instinct" in keeping with the then contemporary parlance. Darwin's treatises, while complex and exploratory, do not reflect the glib shorthand of "survival of the fittest" that has since become commonplace.

Darwin never wrote the "survival of the fittest". Herbert Spencer[4], a contemporary commentator first used this phase.

Instead, Darwin's position appears to reject the supremacy of crass self-interest, focusing instead on a range of human emotions, including sympathy for others, including those beyond our family group or species. In *The Descent of Man*, he wrote:

> *"We are ... impelled to relieve the sufferings of another, in order that our own painful feelings may be at the same time relieved. In like manner we are led to participate in the pleasures of others."*

Darwin's research suggests that humans have evolved to behave compassionately or, at least, that we have the capacity to do so. Recent discoveries in neuroscience and neural-imaging support this biological basis for compassion, but it was Darwin who originally argued that,

> *"[T]hose communities which contained the greatest number of the most sympathetic members would flourish best, and rear the greatest number of offspring".*

ˈThe word compassion is a middle English derivation of the Latin "compati" — to suffer with.

We can experience the positive emotions associated with compassionate action without being immediately repaid by the same individuals we help — these positive emotions breed happiness and more compassionate action.

As I hope to illustrate, compassion can be experienced as a feeling or emotion, it can be triggered by a thought and accompanied by an action: a step beyond sympathy or empathy in seeking to resolve or ease the suffering of others.

Examining compassion from a religious perspective, one finds that all the major world religions and humanistic organisations have described this aspect of the human species in remarkably similar ways — and this has become known as the "Golden Rule". The major world religions, humanist organisations, and a growing body of scientists, all agree that compassion is among the highest human virtues.

The Golden Rule
That one should treat others as one wishes to be treated oneself seems both self-evident and universally accepted as the ethic of reciprocity, yet the evidence suggests that humans struggle to put *compassion into action* even though we are not unique among species in having the capacity and motivation to do so.

Christianity	*All things whatsoever ye would that men should do to you, do ye so to them; for this is the law and the prophets.*
	— Matthew 7:12
Confucianism	*Do not do to others what you would not like yourself. Then there will be no resentment against you, either in the family or in the state.*
	— Analects 12:2
Buddhism	*Hurt not others in ways that you yourself would find hurtful.*
	— Udana-Varga 5,1
Hinduism	*This is the sum of duty; do naught onto others what you would not have them do unto you.*
	— Mahabharata 5,1517
Islam	*None of you believes until he loves for his brother what he loves for himself.*
	— Sunnah, Bukhari and Muslim

Jainism	*A man should wander about treating all creatures as he himself would be treated.* — Sutrakritanga 1.11.33
Judaism	*What is hateful to you, do not do to your fellowman. This is the entire Law; all the rest is commentary.* — Talmud, Shabbat 3id
Sikhism	*As thou deemest thyself, so deem others. I am a stranger to no one; and no one is a stranger to me. Indeed, I am a friend to all.* — Guru Granth Sahib
Taoism	*Regard your neighbor's gain as your gain, and your neighbor's loss as your own loss.* — Tai Shang Kan Yin P'ien
Zoroastrianism	*That nature alone is good which refrains from doing another whatsoever is not good for itself.* — Dadisten-l-dinik, 94,5

Darwin's concern for "compassion for all sentient beings" reminds us that compassion towards animals allows us to experience how much they can give with their own compassionate impulses.

The first poem I have selected introduces us to the phenomenon of compassion in animals and acts as a preface to the more evolved human manifestation of compassion.

A NEW ANIMAL KINGDOM

In the Kingdom of animal royalty
Where cats and dogs would reign
There'd be no sign of cruelty
Nothing inhumane

To join, just sign the application
With paw-prints, you'll prevail
Complete your obligation
With the wagging of your tail
You'll never have to wear a leash
As humans are not allowed
Come and go, just as you please
T'would be the cat's meow

Coyotes and wolves and dogs and cats
All creatures of the night
Like frogs and turtles and owls and bats
Deserve their Bill of Rights

Humans are so certain that
Our planet's their domain
But they also thought the world was flat
How foolishly inane

So join with us in our freedom fight
For animal liberation
As we strive on earth to set things right
Against human domination.

Stanley Cooper[5]

I have chosen some different poems to locate compassion, and I hope this will illustrate the concept much better than any academic explanation:

Proximal Compassion
Distal Compassion
Global Compassion
Self-Compassion
Compassion Fatigue

I will occasionally throughout the book add one of my own favourites. The first is by my colleague in Louisville, Kentucky who spent his career making documentaries for the BBC. It is called "Listening to Understand" and quotes Yogi Berra.

LISTENING TO UNDERSTAND

"It's amazing what you hear when you listen" — Yogi Berra
Do you hear what I hear; do you see what I see:
Is this only Christmas music or can we actually
Hear and see what others see? Is it possible?
What does it take: is it training, hard work,
Both or some supernatural gift?

The real gift comes through
Abandoning listening to respond
And learning to listen to understand.
I learn very little when my lips are moving, except
Perhaps what I already know. How good is that,
Who does it help, unless it is coupled with sharing?
When I listen to understand, I begin to make a human
Connection. A connection which is quickly lost
When I interrupt. If my advice is so valuable
Why do I not take it myself? Why should you
Listen when I talk, what is in it for you?

If I try to understand you, your thoughts can
Improve mine and your chance to be truly heard
Might be a completely new experience for us both.
We both might learn, we might both benefit;
What a novel idea. Active listening is a gift
Of compassion. One can only keep
Compassion by giving it away.
You cannot hoard compassion, you cannot
Stockpile it to save it for a rainy day.
You must actively and purposely give it away
If you want any chance of keeping some for yourself.

John-Robert Curtin[6]

Proximal Compassion

The first concept of compassion is almost certainly the most common and easily understood. It is linked to the word kind or kindness: the word itself derived from the old English *kinde* meaning nature, family, kin ie someone close to us both in lineage (a mother and her baby) or in distance (a beggar we pass on the street). As a species we are driven by tribal loyalty and acts of kindness are more easily evoked — and the emotions more easily stirred — by the plight of our nearest and dearest. The personal and psychological expression of this form of compassion is often determined by whom we accept as our kin. If we are English — how do we feel about the Scottish — or if we feel British — how do we feel about the Germans?

Proximal compassion is experienced emotionally and with some vigour. This biological drive is evoked most strongly between a mother and her young and we share this response with many of our fellow mammals.

The poem I have chosen to illustrate this form of compassion builds on the first read and is called "Ears that Hear" by Gayle McMillan. She writes, "I like to express myself through the artistry of words."

EARS THAT HEAR

Ears that hear, eyes that see,
A heart that understands.
One who sees the broken pieces,
Gently holding them in your hands.

Eyes that tear up with emotion,
Ears that hear what you can't say,
A heart that beats with feeling,
Helping pain to edge away.

Ears that hear the silent cries,
A heart that feels the breaking,
A soul who knows that kind of pain,
The anguish, depth of aching.

Ears that listen patiently,
Eyes that see through tears,
An empathetic, caring heart
That understands your fears

Gabby Mac[7]

Distal Compassion

Distal compassion captures how we respond to something we see on the television or read in the newspaper or hear on the radio. Over Christmas we are often flooded with requests for the famine in Yemen, the plight of the refuges in the Mediterranean — maybe even the numerous food banks in Shropshire — the loneliness of the isolated elderly. Although our response initially may be emotionally driven, we will almost certainly have thought as well about the particular event, and which one would we choose to help. Compassion may drive us to action, and this will often involve our donating to the charity in question. Sometimes the plight of the poor folk we witness may evoke anger as well as sympathy. We may, of course, do nothing.

A poem I was very moved by myself and had it read out at our conference in Shrewsbury in 2015, was written and delivered by Warsan Shire. She is a British writer, born to Somali parents in Kenya. Her poem won the Brunel University African Poetry Prize in 2013.

Excerpted from 'HOME'

... you have to understand,
that no one puts their children in a boat
unless the water is safer than the land
no one burns their palms
under trains
beneath carriages
no one spends days and nights in the stomach of a truck
feeding on newspaper unless the miles travelled
means something more than journey.
no one crawls under fences
no one wants to be beaten
pitied

no one chooses refugee camps
or strip searches where your
body is left aching
or prison,
because prison is safer
than a city of fire
and one prison guard
in the night
is better than a truckload
of men who look like your father
no one could take it
no one could stomach it
no one skin would be tough enough ...

... no one leaves home until home is a sweaty voice in your ear
saying-
leave,
run away from me now
i don't know what i've become
but i know that anywhere
is safer than here

Warsan Shire[8]

Global Compassion

Global compassion: I use this term to describe our relationship to our environment, to nature, to the sky, the sea, the earth, other species. For many other cultures this is the central focus of their lives and shapes and determines how they live. We tend to use the word "primitive" to describe them. I had a sabbatical when I had recently qualified as a doctor and spent my time in the States helping to establish a family medicine service. This was in North Carolina and we were close to a Native American Cherokee tribal area. I spent some time with the local "medicine man" learning how he was trained and worked. In the first week he took me to the forest area and asked me to identify a tree. I was able to say, "That is an oak tree." He asked, "Tell me what you know about oak trees?" I spluttered out the Latin name Quercus, of the beech family, and that there were many different varieties. I had just about reached the end of my knowledge when he said,

"Well, what we learn about oak trees involves which birds go to the oak tree, what happens when there is a fierce wind, and what does the grass look like under the oak tree. You see, you learn about nature in an isolated scientific manner, we learn about how a tree, or it could be a cat or dog, lives alongside the habitat it exists in. you probably know about the cat family and know about tigers or leopards, but when do you see a cat and tiger together? We live alongside our natural environment, you dig it up, want to extract the oil, the gold, the diamonds, and do not really take climate change seriously."

And yes, we now have to take it seriously. The ice is rapidly melting at the North Pole, the coral is disappearing in the South East sea, the air is polluted by our smoke, microplastics are found in the fish we eat — and so on.

Compassion towards our environment, learning to live within it without destroying it is now a major challenge.

The poem I have chosen is called "The Silent Sea" by Rachael Boast, a British poet, and it is from a collection by Carol Ann Duffy on climate change. Rachael won the T. S. Elliot Prize.

SILENT SEA

We were the first that ever burst
Into that silent sea
— ST Coleridge

Another vessel sheds the chrome
of its silver mile until a mile
meanders into three, triples again
over the reef. Nothing can breathe
under oil, nor register that
dark membrane's slick
over sight. We were the first
cracking the hull of the earth
open, our foolish husbandry
a metallurgy that's brimmed
with false gold too often
we can talk, and talk, and talk
but a ship in space, manned
by non-thinking from non-feeling,
says absolutely nothing at all.

Rachael Boast[9]

MOTHER EARTH

Our Earth is beautiful as viewed from the sky.
But wait! Is Mother about to cry?
This blue planet shakes and trembles and sheds its tears
As it feels the wars and the pain of its tenants' fears.
It's the human ones causing the destruction.
Of all that Mother put into production,
Millions of eons shifting lands to and fro,
Forming mountains and valleys and waters that flow,
Habitats grown to nurture all her children
Are destroyed by the greed of human evolution.
Has the Mother taken all that she can?
Is she objecting to the iniquities of man?
How many cuts and incisions can she take?
As species land and forests disappear in man's wake,
She gives her warnings as the elements explode,
Showing how vulnerable humans are in their humble abodes.
Catastrophes are spreading across the globe.
How much worse will they become? No one knows.
The Mother is angry, and she has just begun
To vent her fury as she converses with her sun,
So beware, human ones, and heed Mother's actions.
Let not complacency and avarice become your distractions.
Has the Mother not provided all that you need?
Yet you repay her with ignorance and contempt as you feed,
So open your eyes, human ones, and respect Mother's love,
For this is Mother Earth given to us from above.

Dave Mottram[10]

SELF COMPASSION

It is a truism in mental health work that the art of caring for others is "caring for others" and learning how to care starts with caring for ourselves. Many new words have recently appeared — resilience, mindfulness, stress-awareness, and the book shops are full of "how to" books. In my professional career I have run many such workshops and seminars. My colleague, John Ballatt and his wife Penny Campling have written a book aimed at healthcare workers called *Intelligent Kindness*,[11] which many of us have found invaluable. Our own contribution has been to establish a mentoring programme available to anyone working in the NHS.

Definitions of mentoring vary according to context and intended outcomes. In Western culture the traditional model for mentoring has evolved from the ancient Greek story of how Odysseus left his son in the care of an older wise man, called Mentor, as he set out on his legendary journey. The name mentor then entered the language meaning "a wise and trusted advisor". Traditionally then, in organisations and the professions, a mentor was seen as an older/more senior colleague (usually a man) who would take a more junior colleague (also usually a man) under his wing and advise and support him as his career developed. This was often a relationship based on patronage, where you could expect your mentor, because of his position in the company or profession, to "open doors" for you.

In the past decade mentoring within organisations and the professions has grown and the model itself has evolved. The concept of patronage is now seen as much less desirable in that it often excludes sections of the community and work force (notably women and people from minority ethnic communities). In Europe, though less so in the United States, mentoring is now seen as a formally managed developmental process where the relationship between mentor and mentee is more equal, where there is a clear contract for development and where both parties are recognised as gaining from their involvement.

Where mentoring can help is in providing a time when the mentee can be encouraged to explore how he/she develops the practice of "self-compassion". The list of activities is large, and reading poems is definitely one that many find helpful. Others might include:

Meditation/yoga/Buddhism/Christian prayer etc
Breathing and relaxation
Exercising — jogging/team sport
Long walks/fishing
Retreating to your favourite place
Listening to music
Joining a group of like-minded people

Keeping a diary
Taking care of your diet
Singing in a choir
Learning a new skill — cooking/pottery
Seeking a mentor or trusted friend or counsellor
Gardening
Adopting a pet — cat/dog/horse, etc.

Below are some examples of how poems can be life changing just by reading them. I include some of my own favourites. There is no doubt however that we are all able to cope with the challenges we face if we are supported by another human being who will "bear witness" to our suffering. (See the section on resilience.)

THE BEST MEDICINE

It must be genetic
that just lying on our backs
made me and my brother laugh.
When we had adjoining bedrooms
our mother would shout up the stairs
'Stop reading now and go to sleep'.
Later she would shout again
'Stop laughing now'.

Adult, I went to yoga classes
and at the end we had to lie
on our backs on our mats and relax
doing yogic breathing, but before long
I was asked to leave before that part –
disruptive to meditation.

Come to think of it
lying on my back laughing
has caused me quite a bit of trouble
in the past.

Meg Cox[12]

I WANDERED LONELY AS A CLOUD

I wandered lonely as a cloud
That floats on high o'er vales and hills,
When all at once I saw a crowd,
A host, of golden daffodils;
Beside the lake, beneath the trees,
Fluttering and dancing in the breeze.

Continuous as the stars that shine
And twinkle on the milky way,
They stretched in never-ending line
Along the margin of a bay:
Ten thousand saw I at a glance,
Tossing their heads in sprightly dance.

The waves beside them danced; but they
Out-did the sparkling waves in glee:
A poet could not but be gay,
In such a jocund company:
I gazed—and gazed—but little thought
What wealth the show to me had brought:

For oft, when on my couch I lie
In vacant or in pensive mood,
They flash upon that inward eye
Which is the bliss of solitude;
And then my heart with pleasure fills,
And dances with the daffodils

William Wordsworth[13]

JUST FOR ME

What if a poem were just for me?
What if I were audience enough because I am,
Because this person here is alive, is flesh,
Is conscious, has feelings, counts?
What if this one person mattered not just for what
She can do in the world
But because she is *part* of the world
And has a soft and tender heart?
What if that heart mattered,
if kindness to this one mattered?
What if she were *not* distinct from all others,
But instead connected to others in her sense of being distinct,
    of being alone,
Of being uniquely isolated, the one piece removed from the picture—
All the while vulnerable under, deep under,
    the layers of sedimentary defense.
Oh let me hide
Let me be ultimately great,
Ultimately shy,
Remove me, then I don't have to...
be...
But I am.
Through all the antics of distinctness from others,
    or not-really-there-ness, I remain
No matter what my disguise—
Genius, idiot, gloriousness, scum—
Underneath, it's still just me, still here,
Still warm and breathing and human
With another chance simply to say hi, and recognize my tenderness
And be just a little bit kind to *this* one as well,
Because she counts, too.

Anon[14]

Many poets over the centuries have written moving accounts of their own inner search, some mystically (Rumi), some at length (Milton), some from direct experience St. John on the Cross (*Dark Night of the Soul*). Mary Oliver in this short poem speaks to this journey directly and eloquently.

THE JOURNEY

One day you finally knew
what you had to do, and began,
though the voices around you
kept shouting
their bad advice —
though the whole house
began to tremble
and you felt the old tug
at your ankles.
"Mend my life!"
each voice cried.
But you didn't stop.
You knew what you had to do,
though the wind pried
with its stiff fingers
at the very foundations,
though their melancholy
was terrible.
It was already late
enough, and a wild night,
and the road full of fallen
branches and stones.

But little by little,
as you left their voices behind,
the stars began to burn
through the sheets of clouds,
and there was a new voice
which you slowly
recognized as your own,
that kept you company
as you strode deeper and deeper
into the world,
determined to do
the only thing you could do —
determined to save
the only life you could save.

Mary Oliver[15]

Resilience

This is another new concept that has often been linked to compassion (a reminder — compassion derives from com — pati — to "suffer with"). We all endure and bear the misfortunes and disasters that may arise in our lives (become resilient) if we have access to others who are willing to listen. Compassion involves "bearing witness to someone's suffering", and it is that which helps to build resilience.

The next two poems describe how we may become more compassionate as well as allow ourselves to acknowledge our vulnerability and reach out for compassion from others.

STILL I RISE

You may write me down in history
With your bitter, twisted lies,
You may trod me in the very dirt
But still, like dust, I'll rise.

Does my sassiness upset you?
Why are you beset with gloom?
'Cause I walk like I've got oil wells
Pumping in my living room.

Just like moons and like suns,
With the certainty of tides,
Just like hopes springing high,
Still I'll rise.

Did you want to see me broken?
Bowed head and lowered eyes?
Shoulders falling down like teardrops,
Weakened by my soulful cries?

Does my haughtiness offend you?
Don't you take it awful hard
'Cause I laugh like I've got gold mines
Diggin' in my own backyard.

You may shoot me with your words,
You may cut me with your eyes,
You may kill me with your hatefulness,
But still, like air, I'll rise.

Does my sexiness upset you?
Does it come as a surprise
That I dance like I've got diamonds
At the meeting of my thighs?

Out of the huts of history's shame
I rise
Up from a past that's rooted in pain
I rise
I'm a black ocean, leaping and wide,
Welling and swelling I bear in the tide.

Leaving behind nights of terror and fear
I rise
Into a daybreak that's wondrously clear
I rise
Bringing the gifts that my ancestors gave,
I am the dream and the hope of the slave.
I rise
I rise
I rise.

Maya Angelou[16]

Compassion Fatigue

Compassion fatigue has also become a familiar term. Often shortened to "burn out", it is accompanied by a loss of motivation to help others. It is common not only in health and social care professions but often unnoticed in family members caring for an elderly relative or disabled child — a frequent cause of divorce.

We all were horrified to hear about the problem at Stafford and how the care of some patients was almost criminal. We did not hear too much about the nursing staff, some not even trained as nurses, working alone on a night shift with sometimes 12-16 elderly patients, some needing to use the toilet, others unable to sleep, some shouting out loud for their mothers, others vomiting. There is no way we should expect the practice of compassion or "intelligent kindness" when we fail to provide the support carers need to continue caring.

It is not uncommon for those who are themselves in need of compassion to allow themselves to become "compulsive" carers, as in the next poem.

COMPASSION

You could see it
In her glittering eyes
On her tea steamed cheeks
The things she could never
Would never
Speak of.
So she turned her
Pain and anguish
Into overflowing
Compassion for others

Chrissie Pinney[17]

The next poem describes the experience of a nurse on night shift at a Minneapolis hospital written by Kirstin Laurel — mother of three.

AFFLICTED

It is the night shift, and most of Minneapolis does not know
that tonight a drunk man rolled onto the broken ice
and fell through the Mississippi.
He lies sheltered and warm in the morgue, unidentified.
Behind a dumpster by the Metrodome
a mother blows smoke up to the stars;
she flicks sparks with a lighter
and inside her pipe, a rock of crack glows
before it crumbles into ash
and is taken by the wind.
Another mother waits up for her son;
he was shot in the chest, then pushed out of a fleeing car.
He bleeds on black pavement, exhaust fumes hover over him.
Through the back doors of the ER
medics dump off the indigent
and black-booted cops track in salt and sand.
We are all misplaced.
An Indian brave
is just plain drunk;
the white paint on his cheeks and nose
is from huffing paint.
He is snoring off his stupor
from drinking bottles of Listerine
(the poor man's liquor).

It's so easy to judge
but we are all broken, in one way or another;
The officer was just trying to clean up the streets
keep his back seat sanitary
when he picked up another filthy drunk
and shoved him into the trunk of his squad car.
The young nurse was conned
into being callous;
It only took being spit at, being called a bitch
and one punch to the face, to learn to be gruff
and keep them all cuffed to the bed:
She takes off soiled jeans,
uncovers scraps of a shredded newspaper
the homeless man's underpants (pissed-on words).
A grimy, tattered shirt is stuck to his chest,
she peels it off, holding her breath, while
flakes of dead skin detach into the air.
In one more hour it will be daybreak.
She will go home to her clean house,
her white down comforter on a pillow-topped bed.
But, she knows,
there is an affliction in the air.
Even the snowflakes fall like ash.
She washes her hands.

Kristin Laurel[18]

Finally, this last poem, one of my favourites, challenges us
to "open the door" to our own search.

THE DOOR

Go and open the door.
    Maybe outside there's
    a tree, or a wood,
    a garden,
    or a magic city.

Go and open the door.
    Maybe a dog's rummaging.
    Maybe you'll see a face,
or an eye,
or the picture
    of a picture.

Go and open the door.
    If there's a fog
    it will clear.

Go and open the door.
    Even if there's only
    the darkness ticking,
    even if there's only
    the hollow wind,
    even if
        nothing
            is there.
go and open the door.

At least
there'll be
a draught.

Miroslav Holub[19]

You may be surprised what the draught might bring as well.

Good luck.

Patrick Pietroni

References

1. Darwin, C. (2009. First published 1872). *The Expression of the Emotions in Man and Animals*. London. Penguin Classics.*

2. Darwin, C. (1871). *The Descent of Man*, and *Selection in Relation to Sex*. London. John Murray.*

3. Darwin, C. (2004. First published 1859). *On the Origin of Species by Means of Natural Selection*, or *The Preservation of Favoured Races in the Struggle for Life*. London. Castle Books.*

4. Spencer, H. (1864). *Principles of Biology*. Oxford. Williams and Norgate.*

5. Cooper, S. *A New Animal Kingdom*. Available at www.poemhunter.com/poem/a-new-animal-kingdom (last accessed May 2019).*

6. Curtin, J-R. *Listening to Understand*. Personal communications.*

7. Mac, G. (2016). *Ears that Hear*. Available at www.familyfriendpoems.com/poem/ears-that-hear (last accessed May 2019).

8. Shire, W. (2015). *Home*. Available at www.seekersguidance.org/articles/social-issues/home-warsan-shire (last accessed May 2019).*

9. Boast, R. (2015). *Silent Sea*. Available at www.theguardian.com/environment/2015/may/29/a-climate-change-poem-for-today-silent-sea-by-rachael-boast (last accessed May 2019).*

10. Mottram, D. (2019). *Mother Earth*. Available at www.familyfriend poems.com/poem /mother-earth-12 (last accessed May 2019).

11. Ballatt, J. & Campling, P. (2011). *Intelligent Kindness, Reforming the Culture of Health Care*. London. RCPsych Publications.*

12. Cox, M. The Best Medicine. In: *Looking Over my Shoulder at Sodom*. Cumbria. Grey Hen Press.

13. Wordsworth, W. (1815). *Daffodils*. Available at wordsworth.org.uk/wordsworth/daffodils-and-other-poems/wordsworths-daffodils/ (last accessed May 2019).*

14. Anon. *Just for Me*. Available at https://theselfcompassionproject.com/2015/01/18/just-for-me (last accessed May 2019).*

15. Oliver, M. *The Journey*. Available at www.thepoetryexchange.co.uk/uncategorized/the-journey-by-mary-oliver (last accessed May 2019).*

16. Angelou, M. (1978). Still I Rise. In: *And Still I Rise: A Book of Poems*. New York. Random House.*

17. Pinney, C. *Compassion*. Available at https://chrissiepinney.tumblr.com/post/ 69596965734/compassion-rebuild-series-no-17-compassion (last accessed May 2019).*

18. Laurel, K. (2017). *Afflicted*. Available at https://pulsevoices.org/index.php/archive/poems/999-afflicted (last accessed May 2019).*

19. Miroslav, H. (2006). The Door. *In: Poems Before and After*. Northumberland. Bloodaxe.*

Photo Credits

Richard Hammerton, front cover

Tom Parson, p. 16

Sandy Kumar, p. 18

Kerstin Langenberger, www.arctic-dreams.com, p. 20

Yogi Madhav, p 24

Miguel Bruna, p. 32

Professor Patrick Pietroni

Professor Patrick Pietroni DSc (Hon), FRCP, FRCGP, MFPH, retired from his post as Dean of General Practice at the London University in 2001 following the re-organisation of the London Deanery.

Professor Pietroni has published several books and numerous academic articles. He founded and was editor of the *Journal of Inter-professional Care*, the *International Journal of Cuban Studies,* and the Journal of Psychological Therapies in Primary Care.

In 2013, Professor Pietroni organised a conference in Shrewsbury entitled "Mental Health — How could we do better?" Following this conference he established a steering group of interested senior academics to explore the concept of "compassion", its rigour and relevance in our societies. This led to a launching conference and the establishment of the Darwin Centre Trust (DCT) and the Darwin International Institute for the Study of Compassion (DIISC) in 2015. DIISC was established in December 2015 to act as the operational wing of the newly formed DCT. Spearheaded by Professor Pietroni, the DCT and DIISC are supported and guided by an international group of eminent academics, writers, and thinkers. He is currently the Director of the Centre for the Study of Compassion at University of New Mexico.

Professor Pietroni lives in Shrewsbury, Shropshire, U.K., which is the birth place of Charles Darwin. Professor Pietroni presented his choice of poems at the Annual Darwin Festival in 2019.

Publisher
SF Design, llc / Fresco Books
Albuquerque, New Mexico
frescobooks.com

ISBN: 978-1-934491-72-0